BECOMING AN
INTENTIONAL WIFE

To. My Sister,
Veda
Thank you for believing in
me and this project. I pray
you are blessed between the
journey and the change that
will take place after the
journey.

BECOMING AN INTENTIONAL WIFE

A REAL Wife's Guide to Excellence in Marriage and in Life!

ADRIENNE E. BELL

KS Media and Publishing Company
Chesapeake, Virginia
www.wifeability.com

Contents

ACKNOWLEDGEMENTS

To THE most incredible husband on the planet, Donald Bell, Jr., I am so honored to be your wife. I appreciate the God in you. I am elated that you are absolutely, undeniably in love with God, and I am blessed to be a recipient of the overflow. Our children consider you their champion and we are so blessed to have you as our leader. I honor you and I thank God for the opportunity to show you, moment by moment and day by day, how much I love you...LOVE YOU (TPOL) *wink*.

To Adriana and Donald III: Mommy loves you and I am so proud of your accomplishments. I am so glad to be your mom!

To my mom: Thanks for being a great inspiration and for the wisdom you imparted into me over the years!

To my sister and brother, Gail and Elliott: Thank you for always allowing me to be ME! Gail, thank you for teaching me how to write at just 3 years old. Elliott, thank you for always making me laugh!

To my second parents, Donald and Valerie Bell: Thanks for allowing me to marry your son. I am glad you both are in my life....I love you!

To Reverend Vivian Gary: Thanks for loving me from the very beginning and allowing me to marry your grandson. I love you.

To April, the Editor: Thank you for all of the many hours you invested in assisting me with finishing this book. You are truly anointed to edit and it made my journey and birth as a writer so easy. Thank you!

To my L.A. team: Juan Roberts, Charles Jones and Alexsis Daniel: Thank you for a wonderful photo shoot. I look forward to working with you all on future projects. Thanks for EVERYTHING!

To my mentors, Bishop I.V. and Pastor Bridget Hilliard: Thank you for all that you do!

To Pastor Qwynn Gross and Pastor Felicia Williams, thank you for the prayers and support. Love you both!

To all of my relatives, friends, associates, clients and my Facebook/Twitter family, thank you for the support and for the gentle nudge to take my gift to the next level. God bless!

Lastly, but most importantly, to my Heavenly Father: It is in You that I live, move and have the very breath in my body. Thank you for Your Spirit that helped me to write this book. I pray that You are proud of me and that a great harvest for the Kingdom team will manifest. I love You!

This book is dedicated to my father and biggest fan,

William Pugh.

Daddy, I miss you and will continue to make you proud.
I can only imagine that you are cheering me on from the
bleachers in heaven, and I plan to continue to make you
and God proud!

ALLOW ME TO BE
FOREWORD...

I F you are reading this book with the intention of attempting to "fix" your husband, I encourage you to stop right here. However, if you have decided to read this book because you have a desire to provide excellent care for your spouse, then please continue, because this book was written *especially* for you.

My assignment is to prepare, provoke, and promote excellence in marriage and to teach single women how to prepare for marriage. My assignment is also to coach married women as to how to be intentionally happy; full of peace, with inexplicable joy. The standard of marriage must be raised! Someone has to proclaim that marriage is not a game, an arrangement, a business deal or something fun to do. Marriage is about living an amazing life of making right choices, achieving constant peace, experiencing joy and cultivating an abiding love.

It is such an honor and privilege to share these nuggets of wisdom that I have learned over the years, either by my own personal experience, or from the experience of others. I've heard many young women bubble over with enthusiasm saying, "I want the dress, the cake, the dream wedding!" But I have yet to hear a woman say, BEFORE she becomes a wife, "I want a healthy, vibrant marriage that will last forever."

I refuse to be another statistic of divorce. I am not against divorce, if a woman is being abused or if her husband continually puts her life in danger by having sex with other people outside of the marriage. Besides those examples, however, I truly believe that divorce is absolutely not an option. I am heartbroken at the fact that as weddings increase, divorces also increase. I could quote various statistics and give results of marriage polls and surveys, but the reality is that the institution of marriage is in serious trouble. In today's society, people are getting married and then, when they don't like each other anymore, they simply opt for divorce. I unapologetically declare that divorce is not an option for me. I refuse to invest all of this time, talent, treasure, and tears into this wonderful partnership that I have built with my husband, simply to throw it all away.

As we journey through the pages of this book, I encourage you to highlight the passages that speak to your mind, body, soul and spirit. Allow the wisdom nuggets to resonate your inner being. You have the power to re-write the ending of your love story. Your marriage DOES NOT have to end in divorce; it DOES NOT have to have an expiration date.

Becoming an intentional wife is a moment by moment, day by day journey. Every day you will become stronger and more resilient. I declare that after you finish the journey between these pages, you will never, ever be the same. You will have peace, joy and the ability to make the best choices that an intentional wife can make.

Let's take this intentional journey together...

*Being a wife should not be a burden, but a blessing.
It is definitely a challenge but should
never be a chore.*

INTRODUCTION

HAVE you ever "secretly" thought to yourself, "I think I hate my husband?" Have you ever said to yourself, "I can't do this anymore" or "I never should have married him?" If you've ever felt this way, don't be ashamed, I have too. I am guilty of having many misconceptions about marriage. The following are some examples:

1. After the honeymoon phase it's "normal" for marriage to lose its fire and passion.
2. A husband is supposed to make his wife "happy" and if he doesn't, the woman has the right to leave, cheat, or become emotionally unavailable.
3. A marriage full of arguments and disagreements is normal; therefore, divorce is always an option.
4. A wife should be able to pray to God to MAKE her husband change according to her standards, and then they will live happily ever after.
5. A wife has the option to have sex with her husband on her terms, and if she doesn't feel like it, the husband should be able to get over it without wanting to be fulfilled from another source.

This is not an exhaustive list of misconceptions but these were the most important for me to illuminate. I've discovered that most of the wives with whom I've come in contact are trapped in miserable, mediocre and mundane marriages. My desire is that we no longer talk about having successful marriages, but that we become intentional about *creating* successful marriages.

It was never stressed to me that planning a wedding had absolutely nothing to do with planning a marriage. I learned the hard way that marriage is not about the dress, the cake, the limo or the honeymoon suite. I had no idea when I decided to marry Donald that I signed up to model Christ's love for the Church, His Bride. I didn't fully realize that marriage is full time and must be planned. It was the full time service to Donald for which I was not emotionally ready.

There is comfort in knowing that being intentional is not about being perfect. It's not about being mistake-free or never saying hurtful words. On the contrary, it's about being consistently purposeful in the relationship with the most important person that you claimed, at one point or another, was the best thing that ever happened to you. Marriage is not for the weak or faint of heart. It is not for those who insist on having their own agendas. Instead, it is a competition of who can show the other the most love the most often.

Some wives often proclaim, "Well, it takes TWO!" While this is a valid statement, we must make it our priority to ensure we are doing everything within our power to make the marriage all that it needs to be. The purpose of this book is to inspire every wife, all over the globe, that she no longer has to live a life dreaming of a better marriage life, but that she has the creative power to build the dream life she's always wanted. As we discuss becoming an intentional wife, every woman reading this book will begin to search within herself ways to take her marriage to the next level. My prayer is that she will humbly and willingly admit that it's not about changing her husband, but it's about changing her own perspective.

*If you can change your perspective you
can change your life!*

CHAPTER ONE

BE INTENTIONAL IN PRAYER FOR YOUR MARRIAGE

WOMEN are the only creation that God actually fashioned with His own hands. Eve was created just for Adam in order to help him fulfill his purpose in the earth. And just like Eve, we were born equipped with every virtue needed to help fulfill our role as intentional wives in our marriages.

There are many popular books on the market regarding prayer for your marriage. I've read many of them and attempted to apply the principles that were outlined in them. I must admit that after all of the information that I gained, I was unsuccessful and my marriage was still on the rocks. I prayed for my husband, as the books would tell me to do, but by my motive was all wrong. I would pray for him to change, never mentioning the fact that I had issues that needed to be addressed as well. It seemed as if the more I prayed about my husband, the worse my marriage became. The problem was that I was praying ABOUT my husband but I wasn't praying FOR him. The difference between the two is that when I prayed *about* him, I was telling God all that he wasn't doing and how miserable I was. However, little did I know, I needed to change my strategy because I needed to gain a better understanding of how God operated and how to get my prayers answered.

The most important lesson I learned is that God is not only our Heavenly Father, but He also has a personality. That personality is the Holy Spirit. The Holy Spirit is often equated with excitedly running around the church, "speaking in tongues" or "catching" the Holy Ghost, as if He were a cold or flu. The Holy Spirit is not an "it" but "He." The Holy Spirit is the personality of God. He is the Counselor that Jesus introduced in John 14:26 *"...But the Counselor, the Holy Spirit, whom the Father will send in my name, will teach you all things and will remind you of everything I have said to you..."* He is here to guide us in every aspect of being a wife; when and what to cook, when it's time to be intimate, when your husband is struggling with an issue, and even what you should pray and how you should pray for results. Once I partnered with the Holy Spirit, my journey became easier. I learned to partner with the Holy Spirit by:

1. Acknowledging that He is here to help me and that I am never alone.
2. Asking Him to help me each day and giving Him permission to operate in every aspect of my life.
3. Allowing myself to vent to Him. Instead of talking to my mother, my friends or even to myself, I've learned to tell Him everything and give Him an opportunity to respond. That's what I consider praying.
4. Accepting that He may not change things the way I think He should, but having full confidence that things will change when I do my part.

After partnering with God's Spirit, make it a habit to be confident that the Father hears your prayers. Mark 11:24 declares:

"Therefore I tell you, whatever you ask in prayer, believe that you have received it, and it will be yours." There were many times when God didn't answer my prayer because my heart was all wrong. I was selfish, bitter and operated in un-forgiveness. Once I made a conscious choice to clean up my heart and thoughts towards my marriage as a whole, and my husband in particular, every time I opened my mouth to speak blessings over my husband, God granted me a corresponding blessing because now when I prayed, my heart was right and pure towards my husband. I became more and more intentional as I prayed because I knew if my heart wasn't right, God would not answer me. You can get God's attention just by honoring your husband, especially when you may not feel he deserves it.

We must become intentional about only changing ourselves. Many of us are missing the mark and that is why we are unfulfilled and unhappy. Some of us believe that if our husbands would change their behavior, our marital issues would magically melt away. We must learn to wrap our frustrations in prayer. We must open our mouths and ask God for help. A better marriage doesn't happen overnight, nor does it happen if you do nothing at all. Don't make the mistake, like I did, of becoming upset with God when you make bad choices but didn't first ask His opinion. Don't ignore that "feeling" that you get when you are about to say or do something that can literally alter the course of your marriage. After you've read every book on relationships, marriage, love and sex, you still need God's stamp of approval on your marriage. God's Word is still the final authority on excellence in marriage. He is the manufacturer of your entire being, so you may as well ask Him, "What's next?" Spend time with God daily and pray for grace to wait for change. When God answers your prayer, the answer will always be "yes," "no" or "wait." Pray for wisdom when the answer is "yes," pray for redirection when the answer is "no," and pray for grace when the answer is "wait."

In some cases, no matter how intentional we are in prayer, the marriage still may not work if the husband isn't willing to participate. If your husband expresses no interest in being married to you, let him go. Pray for him but don't beg him. Offer to go to counseling but don't hound him. Offer to be intentional in whatever capacity that will please him according to moral and godly standards. However, if he is adamant about filing for divorce, sign the papers and let him go.

In the event that your husband shows any inkling that he really wants to partner with you in building a successful marriage, then begin to pray FOR your husband first, and then ABOUT you. Ask the Father to show you how to be a better wife to your husband. Some of us think we have to be "superwoman," but we must learn to operate in God's supernatural ability so that He can mentor us as wives to our husbands. Again, stop thinking about what your husband is NOT doing and focus on what YOU can do. If you change your perspective, you can change your life.

THE INTENTIONAL WIFE'S PRAYER

Father, I thank you for helping me to become an intentional wife. I thank you that I enthusiastically accept the challenge of being a wife inspired and ignited for excellence in my marriage to my husband. Holy Spirit, I give you permission to help me become and remain a prepared vessel for my husband's exclusive enjoyment. Thank you Father that I walk in nobility, greatness and endurance. Thank you for the capacity to walk worthy of this awesome and incredible task of being an intentional wife. Help me to always be prepared to meet my husband's needs and the discernment to anticipate what he desires from me, In Jesus' name I pray, amen.

We must make taking better care of our bodies
a lifestyle, not an afterthought.

CHAPTER TWO

BE INTENTIONAL ABOUT YOUR HEALTH

A S I stated in the previous chapter, don't try to be superwoman. Instead, operate in the supernatural. Even with God's help, you still have to be intentional about keeping a healthy, fit body. No one can make you eat right or exercise. Your health is in your hands and you have to be the one to manage it.

You cannot give your family something that you don't have. If you are always tired, how can you operate at an optimum level? Who feels like being intimate when you are simply too tired to think? Who has the energy to wash clothes, care for kids, cook meals and help pay bills when all you can think about is crawling into bed? Sadly, this is the plight of most married women in today's society.

Many women are participating in some type of weight loss campaign, journey or challenge, while some women have simply given up on living a healthier lifestyle, feeling as though their husbands love them just the way they are. Some of us may have the mindset that "I was fat when he met me." While that may be the case, to be an excellent and intentional wife, if you understand that being overweight is dangerous to your health, then why not offer your husband a fit, well-kept body? If your husband needs to lose a few pounds, gently tell him. However, don't complicate things by buying or preparing unhealthy food that may stall both of your weight loss goals.

Don't cut your life short by carrying more weight than your body was made to carry. I became intentional about my weight loss when I turned 30. Not because I was going through some type of crisis, but because I was unhealthy. I had heart issues that were starting to develop and I was addicted to sugar, which I later learned altered my mood drastically. It seems I was only happy when I had something high in sugar, like chocolate candy or ice cream. I was headed down a path of physical destruction.

I took control of my health by accepting the life-long challenge to incorporate the following things in my life:

1. Exercise and foster a healthier environment at work and at home. I started taking the stairs when possible and implementing personal boot camps to bring my weight down. I never went on a diet, but I did change my diet. Each day I try to eat within 2 hours of waking. I attempt to eat every 2 to 3 hours in order to keep my blood sugar levels steady. I notice that I crave sweets when I am thirsty, so I try to drink between 80-100 ounces of water per day. It sounds like a lot but my body loves and needs it. I make a valiant effort to exercise a minimum of 3 days a week, at least 30 to 45 minutes each session. Make a valiant effort to create your own exercise and eating plan. Your body needs the discipline.

2. Elect to make healthier choices. I no longer eat pork or beef because I noticed a shift in my attitude when I ate them. Consider fasting from these items for just 3 days and I promise that you will notice a difference in how you

feel. I didn't stop eating beef or pork for religious reasons; I stopped eating them for fat reasons. I was too fat and I needed to lose weight and eat better. This may not be your story but it was mine. I was an emotional eater so I had to put some guidelines in place to eat for nourishment and not for comfort. Prepare a meal and snack plan for the week to prevent last minute stops at fast-food restaurants.

3. Each night, attempt to get at least 5 to 7 hours of uninterrupted sleep/rest. If you are a new mother that may not be realistic right now, but sleep when the baby sleeps. On my personal journey, I had a really bad habit of staying up past midnight working on projects, but waking up cranky and moody. I wasn't on a particular schedule and that had to change. I had to make a conscious effort to go to bed even if I wasn't sleepy. I found that my attitude was so much better when I had a good night's sleep. I've even learned that I make better decisions after I'm rested. If you aren't doing this, try it and see if you feel better in the morning.

4. Eliminate negative thoughts and people from your life immediately. Your mental health can have a negative effect on your physical health as well. People endure years of mental anguish, private pain and secrets that manifest in deadly diseases down the line. If your life is inundated with drama, your body could manifest it later on. Make an intentional effort to surround yourself with people that make healthier choices, not only with their diets, but with their lives in general.

5. Each day, take a multi-vitamin to help keep your natural energy levels up. B-12 is the vitamin I use to help keep my energy steady throughout the day. I also take Omega 3 and Vitamin D3 to maximize my heart health. Weight loss pills are ok but I wasn't interested in a quick fix. I didn't need a diet pill, I needed discipline. Discipline is a virtue that must be intentionally cultivated. You can take every vitamin or weight loss pill known to man but if you lack discipline, it may show in your behavior. We will talk about managing our emotions in the next chapter.

6. Every year, ensure that your health care provider performs a Pap smear and breast exam. Preventative care is the best care. Don't wait until the pain is unbearable to realize that you were ill all along. You owe it to your husband and family to take preventative measures to care for yourself. There is nothing wrong with sacrificing for your family, but you don't have to forego your health in a valiant effort to be loyal to your family. Ladies, we must take better care of our bodies. Our futures will thank us if we start now.

Some of us are already pretty healthy and have great bodies; however, I've learned that not all thin people are healthy people. You can be thin and still eat all of the wrong things. You may not be genetically predisposed to obesity, but you may still be prone to heart disease or diabetes. The purpose of this chapter is not to focus on being skinny, but being healthy. When you are healthy, you think clearer and make better decisions.

You have the power to become purposely irresistible to your husband, if you aren't already. A man can tell when you don't feel beautiful or attractive. Nothing turns a man off faster than a woman who has no sense of her worth or beauty. Men often struggle with their own self-esteem so it is important that the woman he marries is confident, or at least in pursuit of a better self-image.

My chief desire is to provide first class, five-star care to Donald. I understand that I have to make sure that my body performs at its maximum capacity. I am not perfect, but I have a perfect pursuit to not only look beautiful on the outside, but feel beautiful on the inside. Becoming intentionally healthy starts from within. We must make taking better care of our bodies a lifestyle rather than an afterthought.

NOTE TO SELF:

I am committed to caring for my body through exercise, rest, and maintaining the proper nutrition in order to bless my husband with the overflow of the results.

_____

_____

_____

_____

_____

_____

_____

_____

_____

_____

_____

_____

Becoming emotionally balanced is an event that occurs moment by moment and day by day.

CHAPTER THREE

BE INTENTIONAL ABOUT MANAGING YOUR EMOTIONS

THE hardest lesson to learn about my husband is that even though he is a man, he has feelings just like I do. In some cases, men are even MORE vulnerable than they will ever let on. The portrait of many marriages depicts the wife lacking respect for her husband and the husband lacking the ability to show love to his wife, on a consistent basis.

In an effort to understand my husband better (and men in general), I asked him to share with me the top 10 things men dislike about being married. This isn't an exhaustive list, but what he feels is most important to the men with whom he's come in contact:

1. Lack of sex
2. Complaining or nagging
3. Lack of appreciation
4. Disrespect
5. Jealousy or insecurity
6. Nasty attitudes and dispositions
7. Profane language
8. Smart or snide comments

9. The silent treatment
10. Overspending

I took some time to study this list and initially, I became emotional and exclaimed, "I DON'T DO THAT!" But I had to remember that I ASKED for it. So it was now time to get to work on how to make the institution of marriage stronger by discussing some common, unaddressed issues plaguing marriages across the globe. After some time, I came up with the top 10 reasons women become emotional in response to the above items. Again, this not an exhaustive list but items that I believe worth mentioning:

1. Lack of romance
2. Lack of sensitivity and security
3. Lack of appreciation
4. Disrespect
5. Not showing interest in her
6. Lack of communication
7. Profane language
8. Lack of drive, income or both
9. Not helping with kids or household duties
10. Overspending/hanging out with the guys

Consider asking your husband for his **"Top 10."** Your job is not to become defensive like I did when I initially studied Donald's list, but to allow the list to assist in establishing or strengthening the emotional health of your relationship.

When I decided that I wanted to stop the emotional roller coaster in my life, I had to first learn what my husband's role was in my life. I had so many expectations of him and I became emotional when those expectations weren't met. In an effort to become less emotional and more realistic, I discovered that my husband's role in my life is to:

1. Love me like Christ loves the church.
2. Protect me physically and emotionally.
3. Pray for me and speak words of life to me.
4. Provide for me financially and prepare a secure future for our family.
5. Honor and respect me above all others.
6. Show me how beautiful and valuable I am in public and behind closed doors.
7. Never physically harm me or put me in danger.
8. Establish the discipline plan for our children as I partner with him to enforce it.
9. Make love to me, and only me, with passion and sincerity.
10. Assist me with home responsibilities as we have discussed. (We will talk about discussing household duties in more detail in a later chapter.)

Women often make the declaration that we are emotional beings, but I don't believe that being more emotional gives me the right to be irrational. We have the tendency to complain about everything and there is nothing that our husbands can do right in our eyes. It's a frustrating thing to really want to make the person you love happy but nothing that you say or do is received as such. When I talk to women about managing their emotions, I encourage them to implement these core principles in their lives:

A. **Stop complaining!** If you don't have a solution to the problem, don't blame him for not having one. At this point, your role is to pray that your husband is given a strategic plan. Your job is to be available to execute it. Instead of complaining, meet the need. Instead of being upset because he forgot to take the trash out, just take the trash out! Complaining about the trash won't get it any closer to the door!

B. **Stop yelling!** Chances are, if you have to yell, your argument is probably not that strong anyways. Practice expressing how you feel in a respectable tone. Be respectful even if he is not. Don't yell even if he does. Having a screaming match with your spouse is unproductive and immature. As you are sharing how you feel with your spouse, think "quiet thoughts" as you address him. If you wouldn't yell at your boss, then you definitely shouldn't yell at your husband.

C. **Stay calm!** Whenever something happens that causes you to want to cry, scream, punch, kick, or any other action, don't do anything. Don't say anything that you will regret later on. Wait at least 24 to 48 hours before taking action. I find that when I sleep it off, I feel much better in the morning. Some people say, "Don't go to bed angry." I believe there's no harm in going to bed if you are not ready to take action on the emotion that you are feeling. Give yourself time to process what has taken place. Ask the Holy Spirit for a strategy, and then take appropriate action that will build your marriage and not destroy it from within.

D. **Be humble!** Always remember, you are not perfect so be intentional about not having an attitude. Folding your arms, rolling your neck, putting your hands on your hips or sucking your teeth is not how you show humility. I know it's easier said than done, but focus on changing yourself and pray for grace to wait for him to become the husband you need him to be.

E. **Check yourself!** Always remember that emotions are temporary. A big deal today may become a non-factor tomorrow. Don't allow temporary emotions to cause you a lifetime of pain. No matter how bad it is, it's not worth you losing your peace of mind over.

F. **No profanity!** Using profanity towards your husband is just like poisoning his food. I know that sounds harsh, but there are evil spirits attached to profane language. When profanity is used in your home, it opens the gateway for evil forces to cast a shadow over your home. Think of a time when you gave your husband encouragement in a particular area and it seemed as if he made a 180 degree turn. When you use profane language towards him, it depletes him more than you can ever imagine. No matter how angry you become, please consider refraining from profanity. You are an atmosphere changer so even if he is using profanity, you don't have to join him. You are an intelligent, regal, beautiful creature and you don't need to use profanity to express your pain.

G. **Be specific!** Instead of just telling your husband what he has done wrong, express the need that is going unmet. The "check engine" light of your heart is on because there is a need going unmet. Your feelings on the matter will diminish once the need you have has been addressed.

H. **Drop it!** Move forward and create a culture in your home that you absolutely refuse to be offended. Life is too short to focus on things that may not matter a week from now. Be intentional about disciplining your thoughts, choose your battles and move forward. The battle isn't yours anyways, it belongs to God.

I. **Forgive him!** Don't continue to wash your husband's face with the sins of the past. If you aren't going to forgive him, then leave him. Become the wife that thinks the best first and not the worst.

J. **Grow up!** Sometimes we are way too sensitive. We tend to over analyze, over think, over process and over talk. Don't keep putting yourself in situations that will alter your mood. Don't ask questions when you KNOW the answer will upset you. Just because you are on your monthly cycle does not give you the right to be evil. Having a period doesn't give you the right to be an emotional wreck... PERIOD!

K. **Be available!** Don't emotionally check out. Giving your husband the silent treatment is immature and breeds discontentment. Find an appropriate avenue to address your concerns with your husband by seeking a marriage therapist, connecting with a trusted, tenured couple or simply write him a letter. Sending a text, email or posting on a social networking site may not be the most appropriate way to address emotions. Instead, take a moment to write a handwritten letter. Put a stamp on it, mail it to him, and then allow him to respond. You will feel much better once you have released those emotions. Be emotionally present and invite God's presence into your marriage challenge.

I encourage you to give your emotions an assignment. Don't harbor or hold in how you feel. If you are not ready to discuss how you feel in a rational manner, write it down. Later on, go back and read what you wrote and see if you feel the same way. Always end your journal entry with a prayer. The wonderful thing about God is that nothing you write will surprise Him, since He knows your thoughts well before they are formed in your brain and spoken from your lips, or written with your pen.

Our responsibility as an intentional wife is to stay relevant and current with our husbands' wants, needs and desires. Don't ignore the fact that our husbands need our attention. Some of us are mothers and we feel that the children are the only ones that "need" us, but our husbands need us too. Ignoring him, berating him and downplaying his emotions literally chips away at his manhood. Just because he isn't complaining doesn't mean he isn't hurt by something you did or said.

There is nothing wrong with being emotional but it's all in HOW you are emotional. It's the WHY behind your discontentment and the TIMING of your expressing why you feel the way you do. Don't try to have a "deep" conversation with your husband about your feelings when he is watching the game! Ask your husband when there's a good time to go over a few things with him. Don't say to him **"we need to talk"** because to him, you are really saying **"you need to listen."** Be respectful and strategic about when and how to express your concerns. I didn't realize until recent years that my husband equated love with respect. I saw an immediate change in how he treated me when I began to respect him intentionally and consistently. My role as wife became so much easier when I simply took my time to respond to him and not react when he did something or said something that hurt my feelings.

Be intentional about how you address your husband. Practice listening to your husband's words, but watching his gestures. Pay attention to his body language, not to be suspicious, but to be sensitive as to what he may have trouble articulating. Don't always assume that because he may not be able to articulate his feelings like you that he's lying. Partnering with the Holy Spirit will help you discern between when your husband is hiding something and when he is simply struggling with how to communicate what he's feeling.

Gently encourage your husband not to shut down. Create a safe environment for him to express how he is really feeling without making him feel bad for it later. Instead of asking him "what's wrong," state the following: "Honey, is there a need that I am not fulfilling for you? Is there something you need me to do more or less of?" I guarantee that when you take this course of action, it will take the heat out of the arguments and the sting out of poor decisions.

Allow him to respond. If you find that he doesn't have a response, don't react. Just because you think he's acting like a jerk doesn't mean you should tell him or treat him like one. Ever wonder why your prayers aren't being answered? Our favor from God is wrapped in how we treat our husbands. Proverbs 3:3-4 says, ***"Let love and faithfulness never leave you; bind them around your neck, write them on the tablet of your heart. Then you will win favor and a good name in the sight of God and man."***

Becoming emotionally balanced is an event that occurs moment by moment and day by day. It's a discipline just like eating a healthy diet or working out. It may hurt sometimes, but it's worth it and you will love the results!

NOTE TO SELF:

I choose to intentionally treat my husband the way he needs to be treated, with limitless love, affection and respect in word, thought and deed.

---

*Choose your battles; some things aren't worth
disturbing the peace.*

CHAPTER FOUR

BE INTENTIONAL ABOUT ESTABLISHING PEACE

WE must be intentional about establishing peace in our marriage environments. Peace is usually overlooked during the problem solving process, but if we are honest, peace is what we really want. Peace is not something you just pray for; it is something you have to declare, decree, and then establish in your home. It does not automatically appear but it must be created.

There are **3** ways that peace is created by the words of your mouth, the tone of your voice and the actions you take:

1. What you say to your husband can alter the climate in your home in an instant. Choose your words wisely. Choose words that build him up and not tear him down.

2. How you speak to your husband can alter the mood in your home. Be gentle with your voice. Your husband is not your child; he is the man of the house and should be treated as such. Foster peace by being conscious of how you address him.

3. What do you do when you become upset? Do you yell or

shut down? Every action or reaction should render a peaceable result.

Once peace is established in our homes, it must be protected. Don't take peace for granted because you will miss it when it's gone.

Be intentional about what you will and will not allow in your home. The two of you should sit down and decide those behaviors that are acceptable and unacceptable. Agree on it and stick with it. There is power and safety when a couple can come to an agreement. There is peace when the two of you can come to an agreement on every concern that arises pertaining to the progress and success of your home.

You have more power to establish peace in your home than you realize. You are a wealth of positive energy resources. Negative things may occur, but those things do not have to pollute your marriage environment. Don't spend so much time explaining yourself and defending your point. Instead, find your peace point. It's not about what will make you happy, it's about what will breed the most peace. It's a common thread to think that love is what keeps a marriage together, but in my humble opinion, it is peace. The difference between a discussion and a fight is the thirst for peace. The difference between a divorce and a solution is the quest for peace. The factor between making assumptions and having an understanding is the need for peace. Choose your battles. Some things aren't worth disturbing the peace.

NOTE TO SELF:

I choose to establish and maintain peace in my home. I will intentionally choose my words wisely and never take peace for granted. I create peace moment by moment and day by day.

_____

_____

_____

_____

_____

_____

_____

_____

_____

_____

Trust is a matter of the heart…

CHAPTER FIVE

BE INTENTIONAL ABOUT BUILDING TRUST

BEFORE I begin this segment, I need to share something with you. If you are living with a verbally or physically abusive spouse, this is not the right book for you. In other words, IF your husband told you that he is going to kill you, then you need to believe him. You cannot trust an individual that threatens to take your life. Please put this book down and contact the authorities immediately. I am not an advocate for divorce, but I'd rather you be separated by divorce than by death.

Some marriages have failed due to a multitude of reasons. The most common recorded in court documentation is **"irreconcilable differences."** In other words, **"We just couldn't get along."** It's really sad because some marriages could have been saved if one or both parties were willing to perform a demolition of their current structure and rebuild their marriage from the ground up. Instead, they foreclosed on their marriage and left the property abandoned.

Normally when a person refers to trust in marriage, it is usually discussed in the context of infidelity. If your husband has cheated on you or has the tendency to cheat, it may leave you feeling somewhat apprehensive about his loyalty to you. However, there is still hope for trust to be built within the fabric of your marriage.

The Bible does not tell us to trust our husbands, but it does command us to respect and honor them. Trust is a matter of the heart, but some people think it's a mind thing. I had to learn to trust the heart of God to know that He will never allow me to be in a marriage that HE ordained and I not be able to trust my husband.

As an intentional wife, you possess the power to initiate the rebuilding of your marriage or make your foundation even stronger, by incorporating these pillars of trust:

1. Make healthy communication and genuine trust a tradition in your home. Don't always assume that your husband is trying to hurt you. Assume the best until the worst is displayed.

2. Turn mistakes into lessons and decide that your marriage will succeed. To trust and to be trusted is a learned behavior that starts with the heart. Once you have forgiven and your husband is doing everything he can to be restored to his rightful place with God and with you, forgive him and move forward. Living in the past damages your chances for living in the future.

3. Don't allow resentment or unmet expectations to cause you to forfeit your part of the marriage covenant. Just because he didn't do his part doesn't meant you are exempt from doing yours. Just because he cheated doesn't mean you should.

4. Do not allow stress and worry to creep into your home. Deal with issues as they arrive at the appropriate time. It's better to treat a wound when it's fresh than to wait until it becomes infected.

5. Give your husband permission, NOT pressure, to lead, protect and direct. Your job is to respect him, not to badger him. You may not always agree with your husband but you can always trust the heart of God.

6. Strive to create and maintain a polished marriage, not a perfect one. Perfection is not the absence of mistakes, but the presence of wholeness. Clean up the areas of your life that need your attention, such as debt, or dealing with past hurts, like molestation or the death of a loved one. It's a little easier to trust again when your heart is whole.

7. Forgiving him does not make you weak; it makes you mature and free. Forgive quickly and as often as needed. Some offenses don't require forgiveness but may require self-examination. If you are wrong, then become emotionally trustworthy and admit it.

8. Be aware of your presentation. Most of the time it's not the information that we share, it's the presentation. A lot of the times our husbands don't trust us because we automatically put them on trial and convict them before they've had an opportunity to take the proverbial stand. Our husbands will be more inclined to listen and trust us if we take more time to first listen, instead of jumping to conclusions.

9. Partner with your husband to prepare a "**code of ethics**" about staying out late, spending money, dealing with ex's, etc. Once everything is written out, the trust factor can be built, or rebuilt, since all of the cards are on the table.

10. Understand that because you don't trust him, there is a good chance that he doesn't trust you either. Be careful that what he thinks of you isn't true. Be proactive at keeping your word. If you promised him sex, make sure he gets it.

Every word you speak has the power to build your marriage or tear it down. Your mouth can be a bulldozer right through your marriage. Learn to fashion your words as one of a regal, majestic, powerful being. Accept the challenge to become a wise builder of your home. Your husband is the architect, but you use the materials of patience, love, joy, peace, gentleness, goodness, self-control, kindness and faithfulness to build a home to which you and your husband will enjoy coming.

NOTE TO SELF:

I accept the challenge to become a wise builder of my home.
I will use the materials of love, joy, peace, gentleness, goodness, self-control, kindness and faithfulness to partner with my husband to build and maintain a foundation of trust in our marriage.
I AM an intentional wife!

_____

_____

_____

_____

_____

_____

_____

_____

_____

_____

*Stress and overwhelm cannot consume you
without your participation.*

CHAPTER SIX

BE INTENTIONAL ABOUT SAVING TIME AND MONEY.

THERE are only 1440 minutes in a 24 hour period. Our schedules are inundated with work, school programs, and household duties. It can become frustrating when we have so much to do with seemingly so little time. The reality is, most of us waste a lot of time but we don't realize it until it's too late. Saving time starts in the mind, therefore, we must be intentional about becoming more organized with our time.

Becoming more organized is not about having a perfectly polished home or preparing fancy meals. It's more about relieving the stress that sometimes comes with chronic disorganization. Stress and overwhelm cannot consume you without your participation, therefore, prioritizing your day is the role of the intentional wife. Oftentimes, we become overwhelmed because our priorities are out of alignment. Let's talk about our roles as wives in order for us to become more acquainted with our core priorities:

The Intentional Wife's Job Description

1. Be intentionally in love with God first by talking to Him on a daily basis and reading His love letter to us (the Bible).

2. Be intentional about showing consistent love and respect for our husbands.

3. Be caring and nurturing towards our children (if applicable).

4. Be discreet - our business is our business.

5. Be a lady - refrain from using profanity and/or harsh words to express our frustrations.

6. Be a good housekeeper, scheduling manager, and activities director.

7. Be obedient to our husbands' godly wishes.

8. Be full of good deeds, cooperative and not evil.

9. Be intentionally sexy and sexual.

10. Be intentional in caring for our bodies by eating right and exercising.

Now that we are acquainted with our duties as intentional wives, we have the responsibility to execute our duties with love and honor towards our husbands and our families. We can be the wife that God has called us to be when we are intentional about discovering better ways to live a life on purpose and not haphazardly. Constantly hitting the snooze button each morning is a sure fire way to always be a step behind the rest. In chapter two, we talked about being intentional about our health, and one of the points mentioned was going to bed at a decent hour. I am aware that is easier said than done, but we owe it to ourselves to be more conscious of how we manage our time.

Some of us struggle in the area of time-management; that doesn't make us bad people, just human. When we decide that living an intentional life becomes a priority, then managing our time will become second nature. Changing how we think about time is the key to managing it.

Here are 10 sure fire ways to become more organized and manage your time wisely:

1. Attempt to wake up every day at the same time and go to bed at the same time each night. Try to give yourself at least 5 to 7 hours of sleep.

2. When you awake in the morning, get out of the bed as soon as your alarm goes off. Hitting snooze actually makes you more tired because your body thinks it's being deprived of sleep.

3. Before you start your morning hustle, say a prayer and invite God into your day. His spirit will remind you to do everything that is on the day's agenda.

4. On your morning commute, if you have one, try to listen to a teaching series about marriage or building your faith. You should try to obtain at least 60 minutes of God's Word per day. It's ok if it's broken up into increments. God will speak to you throughout the day to assist you with the events of the day.

5   If you have a washer/dryer at home, try to complete a load a day. Then when the weekend comes, you will actually enjoy the week's end.

6. Each night, make a list of everything you need to accomplish the next day. Try to plan your week, days, months and even a whole year in advance, if possible. This will help you become more organized and reduce the propensity to over schedule.

7. Be a good steward of your time and don't give your husband what's left of it. Be meticulous about scheduling alone time with your husband. He may not say it, but your time alone with him is imperative to the success of your relationship.

8. Set aside 10 uninterrupted minutes of "you time." Pull to the side of the road or lock yourself in the bathroom. It's your time to do whatever makes you feel relaxed and ready for the next task.

9. Prepare meals that are carefully planned and prepared with love and care. Try not to throw your meals together out of duty or frustration. Even a bad plate of food tastes better when it's served with love and good intentions.

10. As a first-class, five-star wife, endeavor to keep a consistently clean home, either by cleaning it yourself or hiring a maid. It is our duty to keep a clean environment. Along with keeping a clean home, be sure to clean YOURSELF.

Make a habit of bathing your body and wearing fragrances that are pleasing to your husband.

Fight the urge to handle your home with a lazy mindset, but handle the affairs of your home with excellence. God is the master of multi-tasking and He has given us the ability to do the same, if we ask Him. Tap into the creativity of the Creator to show you more than one way to get things done. When we truly realize how precious and valuable our time is, we will cherish and protect it more fervently. Your time is just as valuable as your money; if you waste it, you can never get it back.

Being frugal and prudent are virtues of an intentional wife. No matter how much money we make, we still must manage our finances in an intentional manner. There are many books and websites that specifically address handling money in a marriage relationship. The topic of money has so many dynamics when it comes to relationships. Every couple's approach to handling finances varies. Some couples avoid the topic altogether, just to keep the peace. I believe that there are 4 universal rules that apply to managing money in all marriage relationships:

1. Pay your bills timely.
2. Pay your debt quickly.
3. Save your money faithfully.
4. Check your credit report yearly.

Sounds simple, right? Well, some couples can't get past number one because each person has a different perspective about bills, debt and credit. Singles need to make the topic of money a priority once your relationship becomes serious. You don't want to wait until you are married to "work things out" because at that point, it may be too late.

For the rest of us, we can start where we are by making a conscious and intentional decision to be better stewards of our finances. Here are a few tips to help you start your financial overhaul:

1. Create a wealth building attitude with your husband. Change the way you think about money. It is a resource that God uses to fund the events of your life. God is the source and He provides the wisdom needed to make wise decisions about every single purchase you make, no matter how small. He has given you and your husband the power to gain wealth, so ask Him for a plan of action to obtain wealth for your family.

2. There is an art to being frugal: Save more, spend less, bargain shop and use coupons. Being frugal is not about being cheap, but about finding more money to do more of the things you love to do, like shopping and taking vacations. Why pay more when you may be able to pay less?

3. Prepare a budget and stick to it. Finances are so much easier when a financial game plan is put in place. There are websites and books that will give you a game plan that suits your lifestyle. If the plan you choose isn't working for you and your spouse, choose a different game plan. Having an understanding between you and your spouse will make life so much easier.

4. Plan and budget for vacations. Taking vacations is not just about going to an amusement park, spending a lot

of money and going back home. Vacations are a time of reconnection, renewal and refreshing. Getting away from the routine of life can spark new ideas and new vision to be implemented in your regular life. God will allow creative ideas to come, newness to your relationship to develop and a replenishing for you as an intentional wife. Your vacation doesn't have to be two weeks. Even if it's 24 hours, make it a priority to break the routine. Work hard, play hard, pray harder!

5. Give to the poor. When we help the poor, God promises to pay us back. *If you help the poor, you are lending to the Lord - and he will repay you! Proverbs 19:17.* Some people take this lightly, but God helps those who help others. You may not need a financial blessing, but you may need your application to make it to the top of a job recruiter's pile. You may need a mortgage or car loan, so you need favor with a lender. The bottom line is that when you bless someone who is less fortunate than you, God promises to pay you back if you look to Him for a return on your investment. You don't have to search for people to help. If you are willing, God will send them to you. Some people may not have a financial need, but may be poor in spirit. You may be that motivator or encourager to help that person rise from their poor emotional state. Make it your priority to live unselfishly and make helping others a priority. Your finances will be supernaturally blessed. I can testify that when I make things happen for others, God gives back whatever I gave away. Whether it is time, talent or money, He gives it back to me in greater measure.

6. Don't save for a rainy day, save for a rainy year. On average, a person stays unemployed for approximately 6 to 9 months. Incorporate saving as part of your monthly budget; you never know how much your savings will come in handy when your rainy day comes.

7. Don't wait until 5 years before retirement to start thinking about it. Start from where you are currently. You may not have a million dollars saved for retirement, but every little bit helps.

8. If you don't have life insurance, PLEASE make this a priority. Both you and your spouse have the responsibility to financially plan for life after death. This isn't something we really like to think about, but being intentional about life insurance is something that must be done immediately. Some plans are as little as $1.00 per day. Make the investment in your family's future.

9. Estate Planning: Some people think estate planning is for the filthy rich but that's not true. Even if you only have $5.00 in your bank account at the time of death, if no one has been designated to receive that money, it will become the property of the state. In conjunction with obtaining life insurance, have a will prepared or go online and search for no-cost will preparation. Preparing a will for your family is wise and will be appreciated by your loved ones, especially your spouse.

10. Give away at least 10% of your gross income to your local church. If you do not have a church that you regularly

attend, give faithfully to your area community service projects that assist underprivileged kids or homeless initiatives. God promised to bless us immeasurably when we pay our tithes. This can be a very sensitive subject for some couples, so be sure you are both in agreement. Ask God to give you the wisdom and discipline needed to remain consistent with giving away at least 10% of your income. Expect a return on your investment in God's business of helping others. He promised to bless you in return!

Saving time and money go hand in hand. There is a good chance that if you don't learn to manage both time and money, you will inevitably waste them. It is possible for all of us to live a stress free, organized, financially free life. When we become more organized, we automatically decrease our chances of becoming overwhelmed. Stress and overwhelm cannot happen without your participation. You have the power to plan the life you want to have. You have the capacity to eliminate stress, worry and doubt by simply taking a few moments to organize your time, strategize your budget and maximize your life. Ask God to assist you with your role as an intentional wife to accomplish all that you have on your plate with stamina, grace and excellence. You are the best woman for the job and no one can do it better than you!

NOTE TO SELF:

I yield myself to God to give me witty inventions and creative ideas to bring wealth to our family. God has given me the stamina to care for my husband, children, home, extended family and the poor. I will intentionally manage my time and finances. I will always remember that my husband gets first fruits of my time and I will partner with him to establish a wealth building plan for our future. I will not participate in overwhelm or stress. I am equipped to handle the affairs of my home with grace and excellence.

_____

_____

_____

_____

_____

_____

_____

_____

_____

Romance is what you do with your clothes on.
Sex is what you have with
your clothes off.

CHAPTER SEVEN

BE INTENTIONAL ABOUT YOUR SEX LIFE

MOST of us married women are so caught up in all of the things that we have to do for our families that we forget that our husbands still need to feel us sexually. Some men don't feel loved unless they have sex. That doesn't make them weird, that makes them men. Most men need sex like most women need romance. Experiencing orgasm shouldn't only happen in the movies, it's for us—MARRIED WOMEN! Every time your husband puts his hands on you in a sexual manner, you BOTH should experience an orgasm or some level of heightened pleasure.

What are your love making triggers? What turns you on? For me, I enjoy when my husband helps take care of the household duties or sends me sexy messages throughout the day. Your sexual trigger may be something else but whatever it is, take the time to discuss it with your husband.

Just because you enjoyed a sexual position when you were first married doesn't mean you still find it sexually satisfying. If your needs have changed, TELL HIM! I hear some women talk about how boring sex with their husband is but in reality, their needs have changed and they didn't give their husbands the memo! The key to great sex is communication, not tricks! Hanging from the chandelier doesn't make you or your spouse a better lover, communication does. His ego is very fragile, so be careful with the manner in which you express your sexual needs. Also, some men perhaps had other sexual partners prior to marrying you, so he may think that all women like the same thing. Gently encourage him toward what you prefer. God is watching how you handle your husband and will judge you based on your actions toward your husband.

You may not feel that your husband deserves to have sex with you, but it is your duty as a wife. Based on the order of God, you may not respect the man but you must respect the position that he holds as THE man of the house. Respect is not earned, it is given. The world system laments, "You have to earn respect to get respect," but our husbands are due honor because of the position they hold as the heads of our homes. These are the concepts that we don't think about before we marry; however, now that we know better, God will hold us accountable.

Sometimes poor eating habits can alter your sexual appetite, so I encourage you to eat better for better sex. Your body is just like any other machine; if you put junk in it, it will operate like junk is in it. Steer clear of fast-food, too much caffeine and sugar. These things can take a toll on your sex drive.

Create the sex life you want to have and be intentional about having better sex more often. One famous fast-food chain encourages us to eat more chicken. I am encouraging you to HAVE MORE GREAT SEX! Find more intentional ways to WOW your husband in the bedroom. When he seems to be in a bad mood, slip into something sexy and intentionally pursue him sexually. They love when we take charge in the bedroom, occasionally, and sometimes sex is the best therapy for them.

Make eye contact with your husband and gently guide him on how to properly please you emotionally, sexually and relationally.

Accept the challenge to become the chief sexual stimulator for your husband. Don't scold him like a puppy in training, but gently and lovingly guide him with your hands and your strategically placed words to heighten your sexual pleasure.

Oral sex is something about which many Christians debate. Some feel that it's inappropriate, while others feel that what happens in a couple's bedroom is between them and God. I am inclined to believe the latter. If you or your husband believe that oral sex is something that you both enjoy, then by all means, make that a part of your love making. If the two of you have differing opinions about it, don't allow it to keep you from having sex at all. Consider talking to a therapist to discuss why your opinions differ. Not having oral sex is not a reason to get a divorce, but it is worth discussing with a licensed therapist so that a need will not go unmet. The professional should be able to guide you both to a reasonable compromise or redirect you on how oral sex has very little to do with the love you have for your spouse.

Now, if your husband is dealing with some type of erectile dysfunction, seek professional help. If that "blue pill" is what's needed to enhance your sexual experience, by all means, make the investment. If your husband enjoys for you to dress up like a sexy nurse or French maid, by all means, you have the creativity to entertain him like no other woman can. There are hundreds of ways to entertain your husband in the bedroom. The easiest way to find out is to ask him what he likes.

Young wives often ask me how I feel about sex toys, playing dress up, pornographic videos and having orgies from a biblical perspective. The marriage bed was designed to be the most purified of all connections that God has ever created. It is the closest to heaven that we will ever experience. Some couples think its okay to add "props" to their love making sessions but personally, I don't need any outside forces to assist me in reaching my sexual peak. Some women feel that their husbands just can't satisfy them but I've learned that often-times, there is an issue going unaddressed. The thing about using sex toys is that you may not appreciate walking in on your spouse being "one" with the device when you are not in the picture. This sentiment goes hand in hand with pornographic movies. Some feel that it is okay to watch pornographic movies with their husbands. I disagree because most times, the actors in the movies aren't married. Also, having orgies are completely outside of the will of God. Just like the sex toy or pornographic movie, you don't want to walk in and witness your husband being intimate with someone other than you. God created sex for you and your husband to enjoy, so ask Him for a better sexual strategy that is customized for your marriage.

There are so many couples that make the mistake of bringing the past into their sex lives. Some spouses make the mistake of discussing past lovers, both male and female. Wives, and even some men, suffer with mental scars from rape, molestation, divorce and deep emotional scars, such as abandonment due to a loss of a parent or child. Over the years I have learned that some men have difficulty performing in the bedroom because they suffer with an addiction to pornography, they are secretly attracted to men, or they just aren't interested in having sex with their wives. Some men have the tendency to become highly sexual during a mid-life crisis, while some of them have no desire for sex at all. Whatever category your husband is in, you must pray about your sex life too. In chapter 1, we discussed the importance of prayer for your marriage, in general, but it is just as vital to pray for your sex life specifically.

Becoming an intentional wife in the bedroom is not about letting your husband treat you like a doormat or a harlot. Sex with your husband should be mutually beneficial and never one-sided. It is cruel and unusual punishment for a man to make love to his wife while she lies as though against her will. It is absolutely unfair to both of you for every sexual encounter that you have with your husband to be dreadful.

Withholding sex from your spouse is a form of witchcraft. It is manipulation in its highest and sickest form. Withholding is a breeding ground for evil forces to come in and wreak havoc on your relationship. Give your husband options, not ultimatums. An ultimatum is a final demand - "Do this or else." Creating and presenting options to your husband opens up another world of sexual fulfillment through communication.

My husband's voice stimulates me. Not that he necessarily has a deep voice, but it's the things he says that I enjoy. He saturates me with his verbal best and presents me with his physical best when we make love. Whatever your husband does to get you excited and ready for his triumphal entry, let him know! Don't let him waste time going on a sexual scavenger hunt to see if he's found your spot. If he is not doing a good job, it's your fault for not letting him know.

Do not allow your husband to go more than 6 days without a sexual connection with you.

Be specific and create an environment where you both can be honest about what you like, "kiss my neck" or "hold me tight." Remain authentic, stay relevant and don't become outdated when it comes to sex with your husband. Don't let sex become boring or mundane; become the chief romance officer and keep things fresh and spicy. Periodically, create a safe environment to discuss how you can please him more. Don't punish your husband or withhold sex because you are mad at him. Like I said, withholding sex is an act of manipulation or witchcraft. If you are not a witch, don't behave like one.

When there is a mental connection, the emotional connection is ignited. When there is an ignited emotional connection, the marriage bed will be on FIRE!! Every time you make love to your husband you should feel the presence of God. When you and your spouse make love, you should feel safe and loved. Now some may think that sounds too spiritual, but God is the one who created sex, obviously for creation, but He wouldn't have given us a clitoris if He didn't want us to enjoy it! He built you to suit your husband's needs and He has a right to enjoy your body. If you don't feel comfortable being naked in front of your husband, work on your body and mind until you do.

There is nothing taboo about having great sex with your husband, as often as you want for as long as you want. True love making transcends the physical! He is your man, your lover, your knight in shining armor. Your husband needs you to be his chief cheerleader and an expert at meeting his sexual needs. Romance is what you do with your clothes on; sex is what you have with your clothes off. Be mindful of the fact that it's not about having an orgasm every time you and your husband are intimate, but it's about connecting with your man on a spiritual level in a sexual manner. There is power and safety in his connection with you. When your husband enters you, that is the closest you will ever be to him physically, and if it's done right, spiritually.

NOTE TO SELF:

I freely give my body for my husband to enjoy. I will manage my time wisely to never be too tired or too preoccupied to grant him my full sexual and romantic attention, as he is my priority, with God being first. I will pray for wisdom and creativity to forever please my husband.

_____

_____

_____

_____

_____

_____

_____

_____

_____

_____

_____

*Make your home a world of peace, an oasis of romance,
an island of hope, a sea of creativity, a plethora of sex
and an institute of innovation.*

CHAPTER EIGHT

BE INTENTIONALLY EXCITED ABOUT YOUR MARRIAGE

THE overall theme of this book is to encourage you to operate in excellence, in marriage specifically and in life generally. You and your husband must become experts at pleasing each other, as well as intentional about creating a future that both of you want to live in together. You must be personally enthusiastic about your own marriage. Refrain from taking a poll of what's "trending" in other marriages. Being a better leader in your home is vital for the health of your home. Even though your husband is the head of the home, there will be times when you will have to operate as manager, supervisor, coordinator, team lead, and/or event planner, oftentimes simultaneously. God has equipped you to be an expert problem solver and has given you the ability to effectively multi-task.

Be intentional about encouraging your husband as often as possible. Be cautious not to overdo it because you do not want to seem disingenuous. Your words of affirmation should come from the heart. Be careful not to allow any other woman to give your husband more encouragement than you do. Every single word you speak should be one of wisdom, kindness and respect. You must create the marriage life you want to have on purpose. Let your guard down, forgive and move forward. We all have pain that we have experienced, but how much more painful would it be if your husband passed away? Life is too short to be upset, irritated or frustrated about matters that may not be a concern once some time has passed. Someone has to be the bigger person; it may as well be you.

What are the benefits of becoming an intentional wife?

God will give you favor beyond your wildest dreams. He will cause someone to give you preferential treatment just because they see how well you treat your husband. God will begin to perform surgery on your husband's heart and open the eyes of his spirit for better ways to please you. As you make becoming intentional a lifestyle, expect God to supernaturally transform your husband from a passive husband to a forward thinking, forward moving, forward reaching man of purpose and destiny.

Your children will begin to behave differently and operate at optimum levels because you have been intentional about creating a well-balanced, stable and organized home. You will notice that you have more energy to perform your daily duties and sex will be more enjoyable because you know that your intentions aren't to get it over with, but to enjoy every moment of it. You will notice the peace in your home on levels that you never imagined. Take a moment to savor the quietness of peace. Peace is not a sound but an environment; therefore, enjoy the stillness of the peace you've created.

You will find yourself happier because you will know in your heart that you have done everything in your power to be the purposeful wife you were meant to be. You will no longer allow negative people in your "marriage space." Your heart will begin to go out to other women who are miserable in their marriages and at that point, share the changes you've made and the results that have manifested. Take notice that you and your husband will agree more peaceably because you know HOW to disagree without being disagreeable. You know how to have an "argument" without being argumentative. You will no longer have the desire to be "right," but your desire will be to understand and come to an agreeable solution.

You will want to proudly yell from the rooftops that you are happily married. I make no apologies for being happily married, nor for having a husband that loves me unconditionally, and you will be proud too. If you are already blessed to have an intentional husband, then you will run to tell others that they can be intentional in their marriages too.

Becoming an intentional wife won't dissolve the need to want to point out what your husband is NOT doing, but it will give you the opportunity to look at yourself first, and then look to God for assistance at being the first-class wife your husband deserves. Change your perspective about your role as a wife and make his day (and not just on his birthday). Look for ways to excite, surprise and delight him. Sometimes we wives put the pressure on our husbands to make us feel loved, but some of us don't receive what we really need from our husbands because we don't sow it. If you want him to show love, you have to sow love. If you want peace to abound, it must be created. If you want romance to permeate, you have to build the atmosphere. Learn to live in the moment. Don't keep wishing things would be better tomorrow, but live for today. Being intentional is a moment by moment, day by day journey, so you may as well create and enjoy those moments. Choose to possess an intentionally positive attitude even if he doesn't. It may be hard at first. Honestly, there are days I simply don't like my husband and I am sure that the feeling is mutual. You have the power to be first-class even when you'd rather not.

Some of our men are often mean or frustrated because they simply have no idea what they should be doing with their lives, other than paying bills. Partner with the Holy Spirit to show you how to assist him with finding his true purpose; that is where his fulfillment and contentment will be. Something supernatural takes place when your husband knows that you have his back no matter what. Society can be a cruel place for a man, so when he comes home, we are responsible for creating a safe, peaceful environment. If he prefers not being home, ask him what needs to take place to create the environment that he needs after a hard day's work. If you are the sole breadwinner, gently share with him your desires and make no assumptions. All common sense is not common, even if he is your husband.

Become intentional about celebrating personal triumphs. Look for chances not only to grow, but to grow UP! Make it your personal culture to keep your heart filled with wisdom, patience and love as you interact with your husband. I've learned to love my husband the way God does and not the way I think he deserves. We don't get to ration our love or become emotionally unavailable when our needs aren't being met. We must continue to learn how to walk in the highest level of love as is humanly possible. Jesus Christ died on the cross because of His love for us. That's how much love we have to consistently display to our husbands – "the cross" kind of love.

Be available to single women that desire to be married. Give her the gift of knowledge and help her to become prepared for her future husband. You don't have to be engaged to prepare for marriage. We often plan our weddings but rarely do we intentionally and meticulously plan our marriages. Seize every teachable moment to share the positive side of marriage and ways to prevent marriage failure. Don't be guilty of only discussing the downside, but celebrate the benefits of the most wonderful partnership that God has ever created.

Today, start a new chapter in your marriage. Pray and ask the Holy Spirit to help you discern every move to make. Invite your husband to dinner as if it's your first date. Buy him roses or a nice gift. Get to know him all over again. Learn to trust him again or trust him more, if that is the case. Take the time to reboot, renew and revitalize your relationship. During dinner, write down all of his favorite things; you may be surprised to learn something new about him. Don't be afraid to start over. It's okay to call a "truce" in your marriage, so don't be afraid to start over. Even if he is the one who may have caused your relationship to shift, decide to be the one to create a new marriage culture and start afresh.

God has given you the grace to overcome any and all challenges that will arise in your marriage. Be an excellent wife regardless of the less than excellent circumstances. Be world class and not average. Don't do just enough to get by, but go above and beyond providing superior, intentional service to your husband. Marriage is not only about effective communication, financial freedom and great sex, but it's about service. Providing great service to our husbands should be on purpose and habit forming. There will be days that you will not feel like being intentional, but the more you do it, the more you will enjoy it. Anticipate the forces of darkness the moment you decide to become intentional. Evil forces will cause you to think you are wasting your time, but I decree and declare that your best days are ahead and that you and your husband have the power to overcome, together.

Marriage is only boring if you allow it to be so. Connect with other couples who enjoy being married or at the very least, have the heart to want to learn. Every marriage is fixable as long as both parties are intentional. When you are surrounded by other intentional, purposeful individuals, marriage success is inevitable. Carefully build a marriage network surrounded with positive marriage partnerships that will push you to strengthen the bond of your marriage covenant. Seek creative ways to celebrate your marriage with other couples that actively celebrate their marriages or desire to do so. Sponsor events for couples, such as a couple's cook-off, bowl for a cure, or take a couple's cruise. The internet is inundated with events for couples, so the possibilities are endless. Build an accountability network that will allow you the opportunity to vent. Sometimes you just want to get some things off of your chest and that's just fine. Be selective and prayerful as you create a network of individuals that will check you when you are wrong and celebrate you when you do the right thing.

Make your home a world of peace, an oasis of romance, an island of hope, a sea of creativity, a plethora of sex and an institute of innovation. Design or redesign your home into a no blame, no complaining, no profanity, and no procrastinating zone. You are the fragrance of your house and if your attitude smells, your house will smell. You absolutely, positively cannot change the way your husband behaves by manipulating him with mood swings. You have the power to change the atmosphere by being an advocate for love and an agent of peace.

Being intentional not only starts in the mind, but the journey continues throughout your life. Celebrate yourself when you don't react and track your progress in a journal. Ask your husband to help you monitor negative behavior in a loving manner. As your husband, his role is to guide you into becoming a vessel that God can use, not only for His exclusive use, but also for your husband's enjoyment.

My assignment was to prepare single women for an excellent marriage, to provoke married women to realign and reassess their efforts in marriage and lastly, to encourage each woman to promote healthy and mutually beneficial marriages. Let's make a pact to raise the standard of marriage excellence. It's not about being perfect; it's about being whole. It's not about being right; it's about being in agreement. It's not only about being happy, but it's about establishing peace. Let's be in agreement that we will be intentional about living an amazing marriage life, full of right choices, maintaining perpetual peace and experiencing joy while cultivating an abiding love.

About The Author

Adrienne's contract with herself is to reflect the shimmer of God's glory in her natural beauty, as well as in the beauty of holiness. It is her joy and purpose in life to live well, love wholly, serve willingly, and to then leave a legacy. Her quest is to help others experience the birth of their dreams as she tunes her ears to wisdom. She searches for understanding as if to search for unfound money or hidden treasure.

She is a first class wife to Donald Bell, Jr. and a stellar mom to her brilliant and beautiful children, Donald III and Adriana. This intentional woman is a proud daughter, loving sister, and loyal friend.

For prayer requests, questions, comments, complaints, feedback or emotional outbursts, email me: info@wifeability.com